Positive Hypnosis

Other titles by M.A. Payton

*Adventures of a Mainstream Metaphysical Mom:
Choosing Peace of Mind in a World of Diverse Ideas (Book 1)*

*"Soul"utions:
Achieving Financial, Intellectual, Physical, Social,
and Spiritual Balance with Soul*

*Birth Mix Patterns™:
Astrology, Numerology, and Birth Order, and their
Effects on the Past, Present, and Future*

*Birth Mix Patterns™:
Astrology, Numerology, and Birth Order, and their
Effects on Families & Other Groups that Matter*

*Birth Mix Patterns™ and Loving Relationships
using Astrology, Numerology, and Birth Order*

*Healing What's Real:
Expanding Your Personal Power
with Mind Over Matter Techniques*

*More Adventures of a Mainstream Metaphysical Mom:
Finding Peace While Raising Teens, Building a Community,
and Consciously Following-Through (Book 2)*

*Writing Sensorably:
How Expressive and Natural Voice
Advance Recording Thoughts*

Positive Hypnosis
Re-associating with
Solution-based Memories

M. A. Payton, M.A., D.C.H.
Author of
Writing Sensorably, Healing What's Real
and other self-help titles
The Left Side
Asheville, North Carolina

Interior body text is set in 12 point Centar by Pete Masterson, Æonix Publishing Group, www.aeonix.com

Copyright © 2017 by Michelle Payton, M.A., D.C.H. All rights reserved. No part of this book may be reproduced or copied in any form or by any means — graphic, electronic, or mechanical, including photocopying, taping, or information storage and retrieval systems — without written permission from the publisher.

Copyright credits for included materials, see "Sources," page 51.

ISBN 978-0-9719804-9-5 (paperback)
ISBN 978-0-9992426-0-5 (ePub)
LCCN: 2017915331

Published by
The Left Side
Asheville, North Carolina
www.theleftside.com

Printed in the United States of America

Contents

Introduction: What to Expect 7
How the Brain Completes a Learning Cycle 9
When the Learning Cycle is Blocked 12
Learning through Re-association 14
Experiencing Hypnosis, Self-Hypnosis and NLP Every Day 16
Conscious Use of the Learning Cycle to Create
    Positive Results—Re-Associations and Re-Habiting 18
What Memories Count for Problem Solving with
    Hypnosis, Self-Hypnosis, NLP? 20
Staying Focused on Core Need to Create Satisfaction 22
Collecting Positive, Personal, Empirical Data in the Mind 24
What are Past Life Memories and How Can They be
    Used for Problem-Solving? 30
Collapsing Habits 33
Putting All the Steps Together 37
    Step 1—know what I don't want 37
    Step 2—determine what I want 37
    Step 3—small examples pack a powerful punch 38
    Step 4 and 5—see, hear, smell, touch positive memories . . . 39
    Step 6—finalize the core needs chart
        by recording re-habits 42
    Step 7—collapse negative with positive memories 43
Conclusion and Next Steps 49

Sources 51
Definition of Terms 52
About the Author 55
Index 61

Introduction

What to Expect

Positive Hypnosis outlines a solution-based format combining Hypnosis or Self-Hypnosis, Neuro-linguistic Programming anchoring, and related mind over matter concepts. The order, or protocol, of this practice is entrenched in the understanding that the brain learns through re-association of past experiences. Simple ways to manipulate brain mechanics (I use the word manipulate in the most positive sense) will be reviewed with the objective of effectively completing a learning cycle to re-adopt productive habits.

The focus is on the power of remembering versus the power of suggestion; the process is wrapped around the power of re-using what has positively served one in the past. There are countless people that are certain that they don't have any constructive memories, but it's the small experiences (sometimes mere seconds) that can be re-used to re-habit productive patterns. For instance, 70 to 80% of the time spent with clients in any given session is re-finding memories that are the opposite of the problem they want to address. So, if a client is having difficulties with certain types of relationships then the memories that are gathered, initially, are moments experienced in past successful relationships.

The key to tackling this process is patience and following the step-by-step explanations. What seems to be the most surprising to clients experiencing the *Positive Hypnosis* process is the straightforward approach and they already have all the information to solve their problems. More than one client has said, "I knew all that," but lacked a straightforward way of re-using the knowledge in productive ways. The complete follow-through is re-building habits that are no longer serving one's greater good.

So, first, expect to learn about how the brain learns and why blocks occur in a healthy brain. In addition, expect clarity on why re-association is a key to individual re-thinking. Information is shared on how Hypnosis, Self-Hypnosis and Neuro-linguistic Programming are experienced every day to dispel the *woo woo*, perception of being controlled, quack-like-a-duck-on-stage misconceptions. Information on how to collect and re-use memories for problem-solving will be covered, plus methods on how to remain focused on one core need at a time for the best results. Finally, working examples and templates are provided to put all the steps together to complete learning cycles and re-adopt positive habits. Overall, what's vital in any effort to create personal well-being in the mind over matter field is to trust internal knowing.

How the Brain Completes a Learning Cycle

Essentially, the brain isn't necessarily assigning a label or pattern as bad; the mind and body want to be safe. For instance, too much information can create chaos, chaos creates a red flag in the brain, and reasoning through processes shuts down to protect the mind and body. When thinking about machinery, chaos could be similar to a power surge during a thunderstorm. The electrical system can't handle the extra charge, so it shuts down to protect the equipment connected to the outlets. Circling back to the human mind and body, outward movement can show up as doing nothing, or action is taken without reasoning through actions (for instance, fight-flight-freeze reactions are common when reasoning is absent).

Before getting into more detail, it's helpful to understand a simple view of the physiology of learning. Brain research is becoming more and more advanced, but the concept of learning through re-association is a sound one. So, follow along, step-by-step, and the learning cycle will become clearer with each paragraph. For example, right now an action called reading is taking place. The new information goes directly to the back cortex of the brain (literally, the back of one's head) and then drops down to the temporal integrative cortex (I also call this the reflection area of the brain for simplicity) where all experiences are stored. Re-associations are occurring to make sense of every word being absorbed, but revised decisions may not be a part of motor output at the moment; however, data is being gathered and could be re-used day-to-day. The fight-flight-freeze response that is more instinctive when in danger or stressed will be covered in more detail later in the text, but if a person's life is perfect then taking it easy in the back cortex and running on automatic is fine.

It is highly unlikely that anyone reading this book has a perfect life and has nothing more to learn, so I'll begin by saying that it's important to note that putting the word *new* in front of learning cycle would be, technically, incorrect. One either completes a learning cycle, or has no need to complete a learning cycle; life is running on automatic if there is no need to complete a learning cycle. So, moving on to completing a learning cycle, one must be able to access the frontal integrative cortex, but blocks—between the back and front cortex—may keep one from completing the process. Later, steps will be revealed on how to find a passageway between the two, but what's important to know is current research shows that the frontal integrative cortex can only hold 8 to 40 past experiences. The frontal integrative cortex (in the forehead area) is where one problem solves, makes revised decisions, creates revised mental thoughts for future action, and optimizes using left (some may call this detailed, linear information) with right (some may call this big picture, or even creative information) functions. While there may be 40 experiences in the frontal area, another filtering process occurs and only a fraction—maybe 8 memories—will be used to build a different performance, word, or idea to be used at that moment, or in the future.

So, the steps of the learning cycle include:
- experiences being collected—see, hear, feel, taste, and smell,
- those experiences are then stored in the temporal integrative cortex (Reflection area),
- an interest in re-reasoning prompts up to 40 past experiences to move into the frontal integrative cortex,

- and the last step in the learning cycle is motor output (also considered a part of frontal brain area)—where any type of body movement or the decision to make no movement resides.

The key here is that a conscious decision has been made; the learning cycle is completed.

When the Learning Cycle is Blocked

When feeling blocked from effectively thinking through a situation, memories could be anchored in the brain as too chaotic. For example, let's say a parent is being bombarded by her children saying, "Mom, I need... Mom, can you take me... Mom, Jane won't stop hitting me..." and then all of a sudden she can't take it anymore, she has to make it stop. Some might call this fight, flight, or freeze and memories in the back cortex won't be permitted to move into the frontal cortex for rebuilding or re-reasoning, she reacts by saying nothing, walking away, or yelling "STOP!"

The brain is doing what it should do; the brain is protecting itself from overload. Chaos is not connected to recalibrating patterns or completing a learning cycle; overloads like chaos, many times, result in automatic responses associated with quick decisions without reasoning. In other words, just make the event stop! Now! There is no brain space to reason.

James Zull, a professor in biochemistry and biology, explains how to improve human learning in his book, *The Art of Changing the Brain: Enriching the Practice of Teaching by Exploring the Biology of Learning*. I became interested in his work during graduate school to gain a better understanding of how I could elevate my abilities to teach college-level English, but I realized that I could also apply this learning to my wholistic practice as a Hypnosis and Neuro-linguistic Programming professional. As a result, *Positive Hypnosis* integrates the brain learning process with mind over matter techniques.

Figure 1 is a basic graphic depiction of how I interpret brain processing for clients to gain an understanding of how to complete a learning cycle.

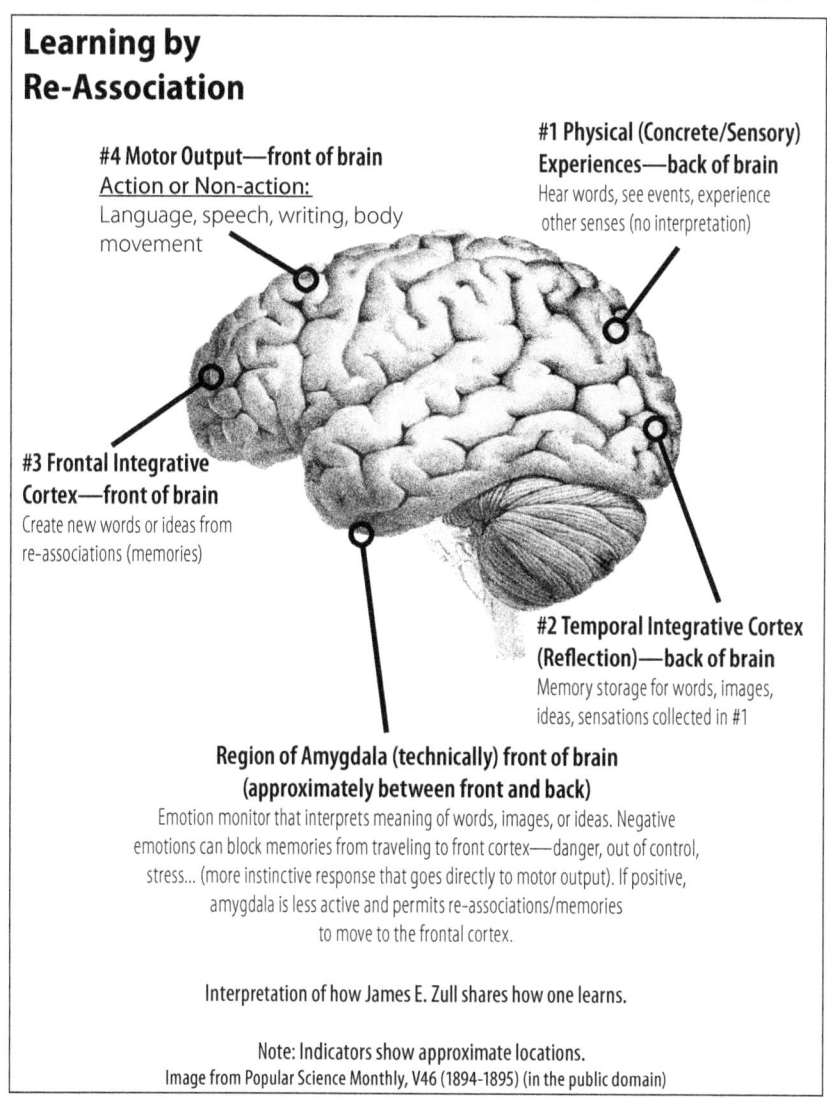

Figure 1. The four steps of how the brain learns through re-association.

Learning through Re-association

Looking at figure 1, set-by-step, when one experiences anything—a word, a sound, a smell, something touching the skin—it goes immediately to the back cortex (#1). In a flash that collected data goes down to the temporal integrative cortex, or reflection area—all memories are stored here, everything is remembered. It could seem like those memories remain buried in the back cortex; these millions of experiences may seem like they were forgotten. But, as one moves through daily life, unconscious information is used to get through any given day. That's okay until there is a need for learning to replace unproductive patterns.

When completing a learning cycle is necessary, memories—also called experiences—must be accessed to use as building blocks to revise behavior. But there is a door between the back and front cortex that keeps information from creating havoc in the brain. One of the major monitors of this door is the amygdala. Essentially, emotions influence thinking and the amygdala is the monitor that assigns instinctive reactions to negative experiences. When instincts kick in then the motor output is the next step as opposed to thinking through a situation by using the frontal integrative cortex.

The reason why it's important to be selective when opening the frontal door between the back and front cortex is the frontal integrative cortex can only hold about 40 experiences at one time. From there, pruning or narrowing down the most effective experiences (from approximately 40 down to about 8) helps to rebuild ideas. If there is a flood of information, or one becomes stressed, fearful, angry, confused… then the frontal lobe is taken out of the equation and the door is closed; the learning cycle is incomplete. Outwardly, the body moves into automatic mode: someone may have a glazed over look; someone may be ready to do battle; someone may run the other way. The key is to understand how to open that door enough to re-reason through habits that re-create the most positive outcomes. So, if re-associations are positive enough to make it past the amygdala to the frontal integrative cortex then motor output will be optimized. Completing all four steps result in the completion of the learning cycle, or put another way, learning by re-association.

Let's touch on re-association a bit more before moving onto the next concept. Individual reflections and perceptions are different from one another. Individuals may get to a similar place—in a work situation, preparing a meal, making wardrobe decisions—but it won't be the exact, same place. Ultimately (and I daresay, luckily), re-associations can be connected enough to create working parts for all involved; it is common to hear the term like-minded (versus exact-minded) used when connections are perceived.

Experiencing Hypnosis, Self-Hypnosis and NLP Every Day

There are perceptions of Hypnosis that are important to dispel when following the *Positive Hypnosis* process. First, some might say that not all people can be hypnotized. When Hypnosis procedures focus on deep sleep techniques to reconnect with memories, this would ring true. But, there are also ways to access memories using Hypnosis or Self-Hypnosis in intervals of trance-like, relaxed states. When looking at ALPHA (relaxed state) brainwaves versus BETA (alert state) brainwaves in figure 2, it's clear that there is more idle space in ALPHA. Those idle or relaxed intervals—miniature trance-like states, essentially—are enough to allow access to memories. When effectively facilitated—independently or with a professional—information can be re-committed to conscious memory, even in ALPHA state (an upcoming section will explain more details on brainwaves, but focus in the key).

The process that I will be explaining further will be referencing the power of re-association in ALPHA state. For clarity, this does not mean that professional facilitators listen to every detail of verbalized experiences; this does mean that clients are consciously re-accessing their past experiences through visualization with the intention of re-learning from themselves. To understand brainwave activity a bit more, figure 2 shows how brainwaves crowd each other in brainwaves—when one is fully alert, the pattern depicts when one is moving in automatic, in the scurry of day-to-day activities. ALPHA brainwaves show a more relaxed pattern—

when one is more relaxed, but not sleeping. THETA and DELTA are slower brainwaves that are associated with sleep state. Common ALPHA examples could be equated to taking a shower, relaxing in the sun, sipping a cup of tea, scenic driving, driving while listening to calming music, walking without speaking... and then a memory suddenly shows up. Sensations, sounds, smells, and visuals may pop into consciousness for no, apparent, reason. When the body and mind are relaxed (but not sleeping) there is a sense of ease and information is more accessible.

A synonymous term to trance-like or various types of relaxed states is Hypnotic state. Trance-like (or Hypnotic) states can be accessed in short intervals when in an ALPHA brainwave mode which means that human beings can, effortlessly, experience flashes of Hypnotic states multiple times per day when relaxed. When combining being relaxed (but not in sleep state), being positively focused, and intentionally re-finding productive memories, it stands to reason that intentionally recollecting those memories can pack a powerful re-use punch!

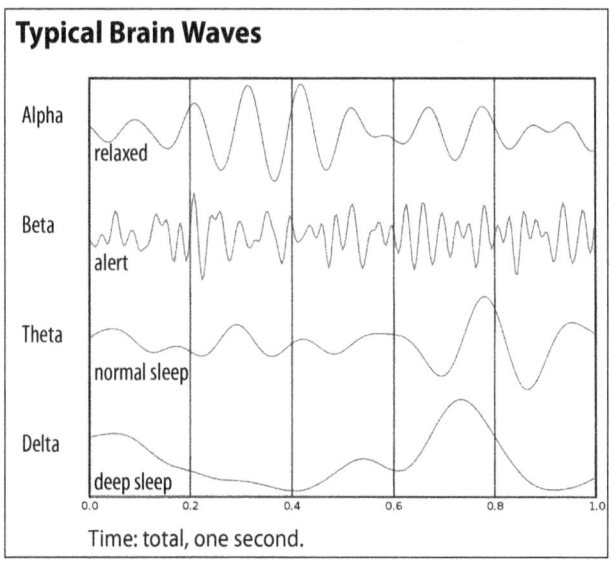

Figure 2. Brainwaves when alert to when in deep sleep in one second intervals (Gamboa).

Conscious Use of the Learning Cycle to Create Positive Results— Re-Associations and Re-Habiting

Let's take a look at positive re-habiting; in this context, re-habiting would be defined as re-using past experiences to re-create positive results. If it's helpful, re-reference figure 1 (Learning by Re-association) for a visual depiction of where each learning element is located in the brain. A simple example would be an interaction with a cat:

1. (back cortex) learning cycle step: see a cat.
2. (back cortex) learning cycle step: store experience of cat in reflection area.

If there is no cause to re-think cats then one goes on with the day. If there is an interest in re-reasoning or re-considering what a cat means then, in a flash, experiences of cats in the reflection area are sorted through:

- Cats create a calming effect when I pet them—no threat, positive.
- I am allergic to cats—threat, negative.
- The last time I pet a cat it bit me—threat, negative.

These experiences are anchors to threat or no threat.

If I want to change my reaction to cats (open the door between the back and front cortex), I must re-associate with past experiences where cats were positive. I will re-use those experiences to remember how I approached cats: put out my hand to let them sniff me instead of moving quickly to pet them, wash my hands after petting to eliminate the allergic reaction, speak softly to keep the cats calm when I'm near them. This will coax the door open between the back and front cortex of the brain to complete a learning cycle, so additional steps would include:

3. (front cortex) learning cycle step: process, no more than 40, re-associations and build new ideas on how to interact positively with cats in the frontal integrative cortex.
4. (front cortex) learning cycle step: motor output, apply new ideas of having more positive interactions with cats, and last step to complete the learning cycle.

Ultimately, new anchors or perceptions on cats are reframed to positive.

What Memories Count for Problem Solving with Hypnosis, Self-Hypnosis, NLP?

Self-Hypnosis and Hypnosis are tools to allow the mind to relax and access subconscious information in the back cortex (the reflection area where memories are stored). Self-Hypnosis is usually referred to when an individual is working alone. Hypnosis is usually a term used when a facilitator is involved. But, when one is in a Hypnosis session with a facilitator, generally speaking, the individual is experiencing both Self-Hypnosis and Hypnosis; the relationship is collaborative between a facilitator and client.

Neuro-linguistic Programming uses techniques that encourage an individual to become conscious of anchors in the mind; those anchors are memories stored in the reflection area. The objective is to re-find optimal habits to enable one to replace habits that no longer please the individual. NLP connects to verbal and non-verbal communication, including tonality—sounds or inflections that reflect meaning. The experiences and the subtleties are expanded and it's not unusual to hear a client say, "It's so weird, but I can remember..."

Now that some basic definitions of Hypnosis, Self-Hypnosis, and Neuro-linguistic Programming have been covered, the next step is to understand how to problem-solve with these mind over matter tools. There are many ways to approach collapsing habits that no longer contribute to one's well-being. The protocol followed in this context is to search for events (memories) that re-create comfort and this is based on finding the opposite of what one does NOT want. Many are quick to say what they don't want, so that is the first re-building block; the search criteria begins with finding themes that are the exact opposite of unwanted patterns.

The goal is to collapse bad with good, unwanted with wanted, anger with happiness. It's not unusual for clients to go in another direction (figuratively) saying, "I want to find out where the problem began." There is a place for that type of professional work, but that is not the focus of the solution-based technique that is being outlined in *Positive Hypnosis*. Instead, most of the time is spent re-collecting successes that replace the unwanted theme. So, first, a person identifies ONE habit or pattern that is unwanted. Identifying only one per session is an absolute necessity, so positive, personal, empirical data is targeted when searching the mind. Returning back to the cat example in the previous section, one sees a cat, re-experiences are collected in the back cortex on what a cat means—positive or negative, and if there is an interest in completing a learning cycle to re-decide a thinking process, the next step is collect information.

Staying Focused on Core Need to Create Satisfaction

Focusing on one core need or theme is imperative and must be established up-front. For example, imagine going to an airport with suitcase in hand, standing at the airline check-in counter and saying, "I want to go on a vacation." The request would be met with a blank stare, or a request to step out of the line and do more research.

Similarly, the mind (or brain) must know which direction to travel. Whether a habit (or re-association) is considered good or bad, the brain is doing its job and taking the road most travelled. How to use re-habits to re-adopt more productive roads will be covered later, but what's important to know now is that three concepts are essential to completing the process overall:

- the core need,
- the re-habits,
- and how one is satisfied as a result of accomplishing the core need and re-habits.

Figure 3 is a graphic depiction of the big picture process using Hypnosis, Self-Hypnosis and Neuro-linguistic Programming, but upon completion of a session each of these circles reveal focused, to the point, verbiage.

The three prongs of an overall session—whether facilitated by a professional or self-facilitated—focus on a productive core need. The satisfaction of achieving the central need can be very basic (simple examples could be happy, in balance, confident, grateful). Memory research to re-habit productive patterns is the most extensive part of the process and will be covered in detail in the next section. A completed example with annotations addressing all three elements in figure 3 will also be shared in the exercises section.

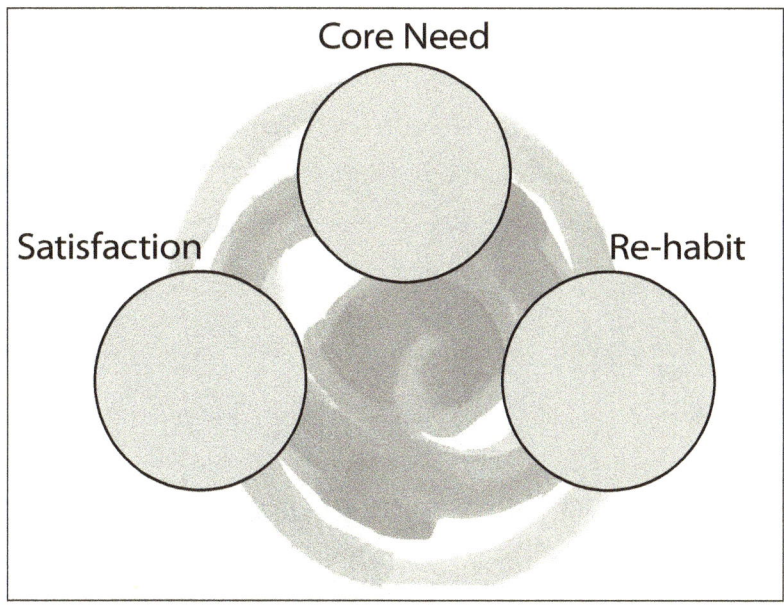

Figure 3. Format focusing on core need, using re-habits (re-associations, also known as memories) to create a level of personal satisfaction.

Collecting Positive, Personal, Empirical Data in the Mind

At the top of figure 3, notice the words "Core Need." This is the spot on the chart where phrases are written down that are the opposite of unwanted patterns; phrases reflect positive core needs. A simulated facilitation will be shared later, but examples include:

- Positive and Authentic Relationships (opposite of unfulfilling relationships)
- Positive Body Image (opposite of negative body perception)
- Productive Relationship with Eating or Drinking (opposite of guilt when eating or drinking, opposite of eating or drinking mindlessly)
- Embrace Productive Emotions (opposite of harboring negative thoughts or emotions)
- Embrace Narratives that Exist (opposite of creating stories and perceptions of possible stories that don't exist)
- Solid Roots in Happiness (opposite of being unhappy)
- Engaged and Engaging (opposite of lack of interest)
- Positive Connection to Alone Time (opposite of the fear of being alone)
- Celebrate the Success of Others (opposite of being jealous or overly competitive)
- Walk in Balance (opposite of being unable to walk without

falling or tripping—medical issues must be taken out of the equation, of course)
- Breathe Easily and Fully (opposite of being shackled to smoking or anxiety)
- Calm with Movement and Sound in Nature (opposite of frightened of snakes, for example)

The key, again, is to keep the core need focused in one area.

The next step is to write a few words connected to memories that achieve that core need—the opposite of what is not wanted. I will say here that many clients will claim, "I have never achieved the opposite… that's why I'm here." This can imply that the client really wants to be fed suggestions rather than search for their own re-associations (I have heard, more than once, "I wish you could just hypnotize me and tell me what to do"). Suggesting solutions before gathering re-associations is giving answers from another person's perspective, but the task here is for one to re-associate with bad to know what a re-association of good looks like; to know bad relationships one must know (or, at least, have a glimpse of) good relationships; to know poor engagement one must know productive engagement.

These re-associated experiences show up in seconds and are, generally, not big aha moments. There are times when those moments are so small that it takes intentional mind-editing to stop the "yeah, but…" phase ("yeah, but then it all went to crap"). Facilitators are a great tool to cut clients off from the "yeah, but" transitions, but mind-editing can also be achieved alone with focus. The message is to choose re-association snippets to remember how that path was successfully travelled. For example, if someone is perfecting having positive boundaries there may be five steps that are working. The next challenge is to link other positive re-associations to build an effective final result.

To set up the following simulation, let's say that a client is having a difficult time with being an enabler; in other words, the client has a difficult time saying "no." The pattern becomes more emotionally incapacitating when loaning $1,500 to people on two separate occasions and the client is never repaid. Others continue to approach the client for money and responding "no" has been a challenge. The client must create positive boundaries.

One way to collect positive personal data on a core need is to create a chart (like figure 4). Jot down 25 words or less, at first, for each recalled experience. The recollection, under "General" (where the initial experience is remembered, but not in complete detail), should begin to take form like the following:

Core Need: Positive Boundaries
General (Short Narrative)

1. The day I, finally, take ownership in my enabler personality the second time someone borrows $1500 and never pays it back.
2. I, finally, have positive self-boundaries and I don't offer money to someone who says, "If I just had $500 then I could…" (implying that I should loan the money).
3. I say, "no" in a kind tone and don't feel the need to further explain my position when a colleague asks if I can fund a professional effort.

The third step is to identify NLP anchors for each experience under the "Detail" section. Summarizing an experience in a few keywords stimulates recall of each positive experience (see "Anchor =" in the following table).

Lastly, re-experience with all senses, usually with eyes closed, each memory. Visualize positive achievements in detail—amplify seeing, hearing, smelling, touching, and feeling. The short anchor is a way to re-establish that the brain should habituate (become accustomed to re-using) past patterns to re-create success today. If self-facilitating, recording the full experiences out loud and re-listening to them could be helpful, but the short anchor serves as a reminder to the brain to re-travel to the specific memory (instead of re-listening to a full recording). With an experienced facilitator, there is less of a need for recording since senses are coaxed out and elevated. The facilitator rarely needs to hear all the spoken words, but will need to record general context to make sure memory searches remain on track and anchor words are recorded for later recall of the experiences. In addition, emotional connections are written down (where an experience is felt in the body, what types of emotions come up), so that those positive experiences can be heightened to collapse unproductive habits. Details might include the following:

Core Need: Positive Boundaries
Detail (Re-experience Short Narratives With Heightened Senses)

1.	Anchor = I take ownership as an enabler, $1500	What do I feel at the exact moment when I take ownership in over-helping? Where am I at that moment? Where do I feel this in my body? Are there other sensations that I recall when I let go of the idea that I will never get paid back? What positive ideas do I adopt from this experience?

2.	Anchor = I don't offer $500		I remain quiet when "X" says, "If I just had $500 then I could…" How does remaining quiet feel? Where am I sitting or standing? How is the atmosphere? How does this feel in my body? What is my body language? What is my tonality? What other senses can I remember? When do I feel positive about this?
3.	Anchor = Kind No		I say, "no" in a kind tone and don't feel the need to further explain my position on why. What is my tone? How does this feel in my body? How does it feel when I say nothing else? How does this feel in my body? Where am I (physically)? What other sensations or sounds can I remember at that moment? When do I feel positive about this experience?

An important note is when remaining focused, ALPHA brainwaves can be slipped into naturally—remember that ALPHA brainwaves are achieved daily. When facilitators are a part of the mix, various techniques to create calm to access memories may result in more experiences collected (since professionals have more familiarity with the process), but self-facilitating can be just as impactful when hand-writing, typing, voice recording, or voice texting. Enhance self-facilitations by slipping into natural ALPHA states while drinking a cup of tea with classical music, sitting (undisturbed) under a favorite tree, walking in the mountains, or lounging at the beach. A question to keep in mind is, "When did I catch a glimpse of achieving my core need?"

Again, memories are imperfect. As long as there are emotional charges to memories, they will be useful and re-believable. The point is that one re-learns from oneself, from one's own perspective.

Core Need:

General/Quick Experiences

1		
2		
3		
4		
5		
6		
7		
8		
9		
10		

Detailed Experiences

1		
2		
3		
4		
5		
6		
7		
8		
9		
10		

Figure 4. Collecting Positive, Personal, Empirical Data Chart.

What are Past Life Memories and How Can They be Used for Problem-Solving?

Some are not interested in Past Lives, while others are very interested in understanding how Past Life Regression could fit into the *Positive Hypnosis* process. But, the question becomes, "What is Past Life Regression?" On a personal note, I'm going to explain my journey on the subject of Past Lives.

When I was in my 30's, I began to question spirituality. I searched for answers in books on Past Life Regression, received Past Life Regression (psychic readings), and realized when I was having Past Life dreams (of course, I had them all along, but I just lacked the awareness). I decided, as a professional, to study with Brian Weiss (an American Psychiatrist, Hypnotherapist, Author who specializes in Past Life Regression and Future Life Progression) for continuing education units at the Omega Center to understand the protocol connected to Past Life Regression and began to offer this concept in my private practice. However, as time went on I became less interested in facilitating clients to simply re-experience Past Lives because once we were finished with our sessions, many would ask, "Are these truly my past lives? ...What do I do with this knowledge now?" Essentially, I realized that I didn't want to spend time proving that Past Lives existed, but I did want clients to know how they could use Past Lives knowledge to problem-solve in a timely and focused fashion.

So, when Past Life Regression is used as a focused, problem-solving tool, what is important to understand in the *Positive Hypnosis* context is as long as places in history (where physical bodies and places are unknown in the clients' current form) have emotional charges, they can be re-used as tools to collapse unwanted patterns in a current lifetime. However, Past Life Regressions could be:

- true Past Lives that have been experienced by clients,
- familial memories that have been buried in clients' DNA (stories told by family, or information is simply buried in DNA),
- or they are places in history that create vibrant enough narratives to have emotional charges.

When including Past Lives with *Positive Hypnosis*, the objective is to use Past Lives information in the same way that current lives are utilized; all memories are used to re-adopt habits that create positive outcomes. Memory research, in general, equates to positive memories that help collapse negative habits in a current lifetime. Those who prefer finding traumatic past life experiences to explain negative patterns in a current lifetime would seek another type of practice.

It's not to say that a session could not revolve around the idea that certain Past Lives are creating despair in a current lifetime, but the lion share of a session within the confines of a positive collection process would focus on strong, encouraging memories to collapse the crippling effects of memories of despair. The objective is to have clients walk out of sessions feeling enlightened and optimistic, so when clients request Past Life Regression sessions they are interviewed on what problems they want to solve. If clients are interested in finding out *if* they have experienced Past Lives then they are given a number of websites to explore professionals who use various tools to allow clients to search their memories. If clients are more goal-oriented on solving specific issues, and would like Past Life Regression to be a part of the mix, then current and past life information are collected in sessions.

Collapsing Habits

Once positive memories are gathered on a specific theme, it's time to increase comfort (create feelings of satisfaction) by flattening out the effects of negative experiences. Collapsing is a term that is commonly used in Neuro-linguistic Programming and the execution will vary from professional-to-professional. As a parent of three (now grown) children, I equate NLP collapsing to giving my children choices when they were small. If one reached for an electrical outlet, the best approach was to draw attention away from the electrical outlet to the shiny toy in my hand. The T-Map is a visual example (see figure 5) of what I might utilize in a session.

Problem	Solution
Electrical outlet	Shiny toy

Figure 5. Problem-Solution T-Map, Electrical Outlet.

The T-Map will only be used after collecting many positive re-associations on a specific theme; this would be the first time in the session (completing about 70% of the session time) when problems or negatives become the focus. To ease into the collapsing process of creating comfort with negative experiences, begin by approaching issues that rank four or less on emotional duress out of 10. This calls for individual judgment much like when going to the doctor and the question is asked, "How bad is your pain? Rank it from zero to 10."

Using an electrical outlet example, adults know that the problem is the danger of being electrocuted, but a child lacks awareness or experience and views this as a play thing. Completing a learning cycle by creating pain (like electric shock) is a bad idea, so to redirect behavior a parent could show the child a toy that tantalizes many senses; the toy could have many colors, could make noise, and could have holes to put objects into. The bigger picture here is the solution (shiny toy) pleases more senses than the problem (electrical outlet).

Returning to the "Collecting Positive, Personal, Empirical Data in the Mind" section, re-association solutions were re-experienced in great detail. Senses were accelerated (see, hear, taste, smell, touch) while in ALPHA state to remember how one moved through situations that created positive results. So, in a facilitated or self-facilitated session, a negative memory would be recalled and a highly, re-experienced, positive memory would be recalled in great detail.

Moving to another example, figure 6 shows a problem or negative memory ("Excessive Helping") that could be ranked a three. A narrative could be that a friend is going on and on about how great it would be if I could lend her a substantial amount of money. Being too helpful to the point of enabling, I lend her the money and she never pays me back.

Re-associating with positive, past experiences, I decide to remain quiet when someone is saying to me, "All I need is $500 and I can get…" I recall the setting and amp up all my senses to re-create a solid memory (sitting at a table, outside, in the spring, feeling the wind, hearing traffic, remembering my meal). I recall how I sit and listen for a short time, but then I change the subject. I remember being resolute (saying in my mind) that offering up the money is excessive on my part. I am pleased with myself. Notice how I intentionally keep the experience in the present tense, like it is happening right now.

Problem	Solution
Excessive Help	Remain Quiet $500

Figure 6. Excessive Helping, Problem-Solution T-Map.

Remembering is imperfect, but it can be close enough to get results. Here's how a simulated-facilitation might sound:

(Facilitator) "Rank 'excessive helping' from zero to 10."

(Client) "Three."

(Facilitator) "Okay. Verbalize the problem experience or think about it in your mind. I don't need to hear the explanation of your experience if you prefer not to share."

(Client) Silence and client remembers.

(Facilitator) "Now. Go to the 'remain quiet' memory. Amp this experience up; remember where you are, what you are eating, what type of day it is… Remember how wonderful you feel when you listen, change the subject, and how happy you are with yourself for showing moderation when helping."

(Client) Silence and client remembers.

(Facilitator) "Now. Notice how this feels in the body. Where do you feel the relief?"

(Client) "In my stomach. It feels like I have butterflies because I'm so happy that I don't have to take extra steps, stress, and regret for over-helping."

(Facilitator) "Excellent. Go back to the 'excessive helping' memory. Stay on that specific example only. Now move quickly and re-experience, in detail, 'remain quiet'."

(Client) Silence and client remembers.

(Facilitator) "Go back to the problem. Now experience the solution in great detail."

(Client) Silence and client remembers.

(Facilitator) "Now. Re-experience that specific problem in as much detail as possible. Give me a number on the specific 'excessive helping' problem."

(Client pauses, thinks, and responds) "It feels like a one now."

Again, this is a simulation of a facilitator-client experience, but it demonstrates the final step in the process of collapsing emotional duress by re-associating with more productive memories. When self-facilitating, manage self-expectations by gaining clarity on the entire process beginning with the core need (focus or theme) to the collapsing phase. The next section will be organized in the order of a complete, formal session to assemble all the pieces.

Putting All the Steps Together

There are techniques that suggest if one knows where trauma begins then the problem can be solved, but more time is required (usually multiple sessions) and when traumatic events are re-found trained professionals should be involved to minimize emotional duress. Searching for positive reinforcement upfront strengthens resolve in a shorter timeframe (one session, for approximately two hours, is common) and is uplifting immediately. Overall, one is looking at the bright side of life to overshadow the negative. The following is a simulation of how a session could play out step-by-step.

Step 1—know what I don't want
Many begin by identifying what they don't want. One might say, "I am so anxious about…" and share a perception of what could, maybe, possibly happen. In this case, anxiety and judgments are built around perceptions that are rarely supported by solid evidence.

Step 2—determine what I want
Once negative emotions are identified, the core need is narrowed down to the opposite of the specific, unwanted pattern that comes from embracing the negative reality. (The duress will be collapsed by the end of the session and will be demonstrated later in the section.) The positive approach is remembered most effectively when narrowed down to a few words and

written down; in this case, embracing only narratives that exist would be the focus. For crystal clarity, focus must remain on one theme to yield the best results. Step 2 is not suggesting a solution; step 2 is preparing to re-associate with solution-based memories.

The core need graphic begins to take shape in figure 7 after the focus is determined. The core need is embracing narratives that exist and accomplishing the need creates a feeling of peace (less anxious due to less time spent on creating stories based on assumptions). In other words, once the core need is adopted, overall satisfaction is achieved.

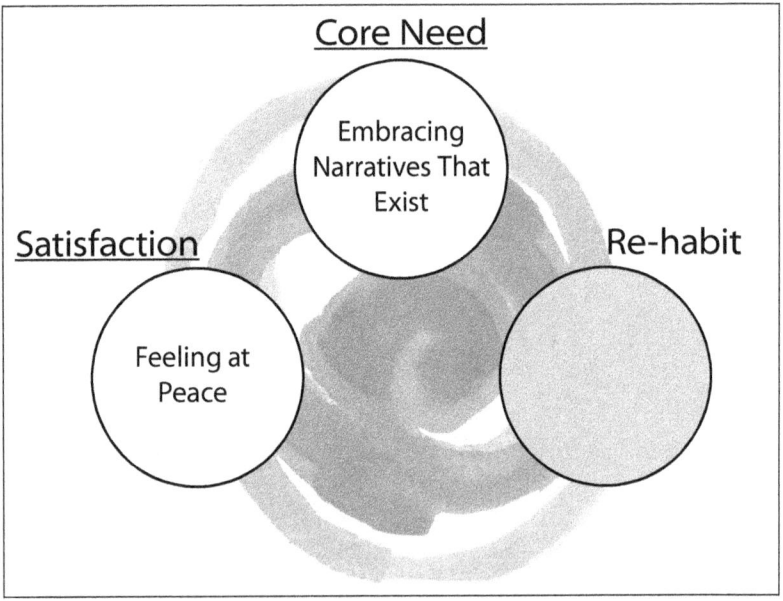

Figure 7. Core Need and Satisfaction graphic: Embracing Narratives that Exist.

STEP 3—SMALL EXAMPLES PACK A POWERFUL PUNCH

The next step is to identify small examples when the truth was clear—narratives (or stories) were accurate.

GENERAL (SHORT NARRATIVE)

1. An older woman, dressed simply, is talking to herself on a park bench. I get a bit closer and realize that she is the Ph.D. that I will be hearing at the conference I'm attending and she is practicing her speech.

2. A business colleague seems easily irritated, so I begin to develop a narrative in my mind (creating stress) that I will no longer be working for the institution in the near future as a result. The colleague leaves the company and I continue to hold a position in the company.

3. I put myself down—"I don't think people think very highly of me at times when…"—and the person replies, "Really? That's not my perception at all." This is when I make a personal pact that I have to stop drawing these types of conclusions about myself.

STEP 4 AND 5—SEE, HEAR, SMELL, TOUCH POSITIVE MEMORIES

The fourth step is to identify anchors with just a few words for each experience under the "Detail" section for easy and quick recall in the future (see "Anchor =" in the following table). The fifth step is to re-experience events with all senses, usually with eyes closed.

DETAIL (RE-EXPERIENCE SHORT NARRATIVES WITH ALL SENSES)

1.	Anchor = Ph.D. Practicing	Remember when I realize that this woman is an accomplished Ph.D. and how I expand from this learning. What do I hear? What are the outdoor conditions? How does the woman's voice sound? Where do I feel this in my body when I come to this realization? How does my body language change? What else do I see? Are there any smells that I remember? When do I decide this is great learning for future experiences?
2.	Anchor = I'm still standin'	Reflect on realizing that I spend a lot of time needlessly stressing about something that doesn't happen. Experience the freedom of stopping this narrative. Where does that show up in the body? What is my body language and tonality when I say, "Only spend time on narratives that exist."
3.	Anchor = Create Positive Conclusions	Recall when I say to my husband, "I will stop creating stories about myself that don't exist." Where am I, physically? Where do I feel this in my body? What other sensory experiences am I having at the moment?

Figure 8 is the type of format that I use when facilitating sessions. Keeping concise notes (one page) creates an easy, visual reference chart. In the detail notes, for each experience, make sure that a one to three word summary is recorded (for instance, "Create Positive Conclusions"), some keywords on sensory experiences are recorded on paper (in the kitchen, dinner is cooking, hear husband say…), and check in with the body (it's easier to breathe, jaw is relaxed, tongue is touching the pallet). Notice patterns emerge with positive experiences; in general, the mind and body know and give cues regularly.

Core Need: Embracing Narratives that Exist

General/Quick Experiences

1		An older woman, dressed simply, is talking to herself on a park bench. I get a bit closer and realize that she is a Ph.D. that I will be hearing at the conference I'm attending and she is practicing her speech.
2		A business colleague seems easily irritated, so I begin to develop a narrative in my mind (creating stress) that I will no longer be working for the institution in the near future as a result. The colleague leaves the company adn I continue to hold a position in the company.
3		I put myself down—"I don't think people think very highly of me at times when…"—and the person replies, "Really? That's not my perception at all." This is when I make a personal pact that I have to stop drawing these types of conclusions about myself.
4		
5		
6		

Detailed Experiences

1	Anchor= Ph.D. Practicing	Remember when I realze that this woman is an accomplished Ph.D. and how I expand from this learning. What do I hear? …
2	Anchor= I'm still standing	Reflect on realizing that I spend a lot of time needlessly stressing about something that doesn't happen. Experience the freedom of stopping this narrative …
3	Anchor= Create Positive Conclusions	Recall when I say to my husband, "I will stop creating stories about myself that don't exist." …
4		
5		
6		

Figure 8. One page chart that documents general and detailed experiences.

The key to positive re-experiences is to get as close as possible to re-building memories to re-create positive emotional charges. These recollections are imperfect, but they can be re-used to collapse negative habits that will be discussed in the next step.

Step 6—finalize the core needs chart by recording re-habits

While three examples were provided in steps 3 through 5, consider gathering 6 or more experiences. It's common that once the general experiences are collected that other detailed examples are recalled—there may be three general experiences that morph into 6 distinct experiences that connect to the core need. For instance, as I remember talking to my husband about creating positive conclusions I recall when I stop myself from thinking that I am doing something to make someone irritated in another situation. I stop myself from spinning another story that doesn't exist and the experience becomes a separate line item to expand on later.

By the end of step 6, it's time to fill in the core needs chart. The re-habit section is a summary of positive memories that will be re-used to re-create satisfaction as seen in figure 9. All experiences could be recorded on this template, or the experiences that were most vivid and uplifting could be added (it's common that some experiences are more impactful and clear than others).

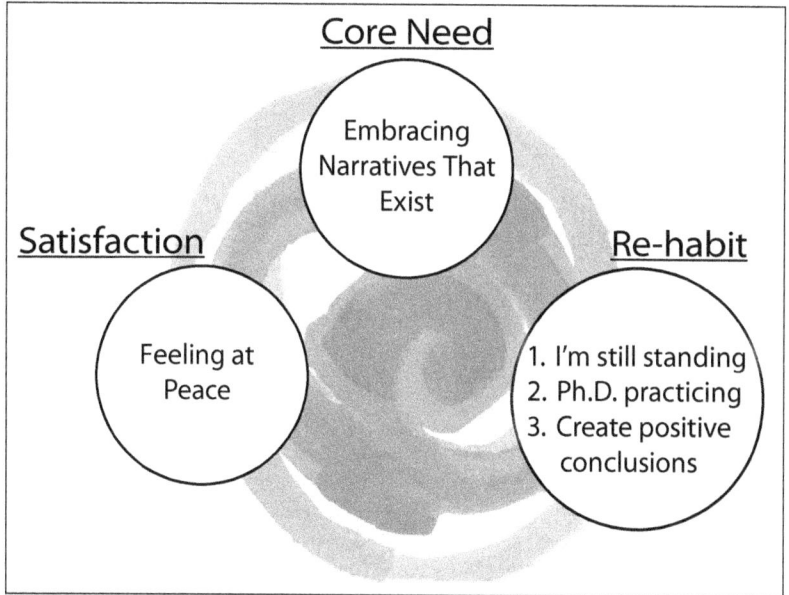

Figure 9. Filling in Re-Habits on Core Need Chart.

STEP 7—COLLAPSE NEGATIVE WITH POSITIVE MEMORIES

Before tackling the seventh step, most notice an increased lightness—a feeling of being free, relaxed breathing patterns, and comfortable body sensations. It could be similar to the feeling of lightness when hearing a great song, or being in a place that feels supportive and comfortable. Taking the time to savor this positive state of mind for a self-determined amount of time increases the willpower that is required for the last step; the last step is when negative experiences are re-experienced.

The most effective way to begin the collapsing step is to tackle less intense negative experiences connected to, in this simulated scenario, creating stories (narratives) that don't exist. There is an intuitive element to the ranking of emotional trauma that is much like one would experience when going to the doctor's office; patients are asked "What's your level of pain?" They make intuitive guesses by pointing out the level of pain as shown in figure 10.

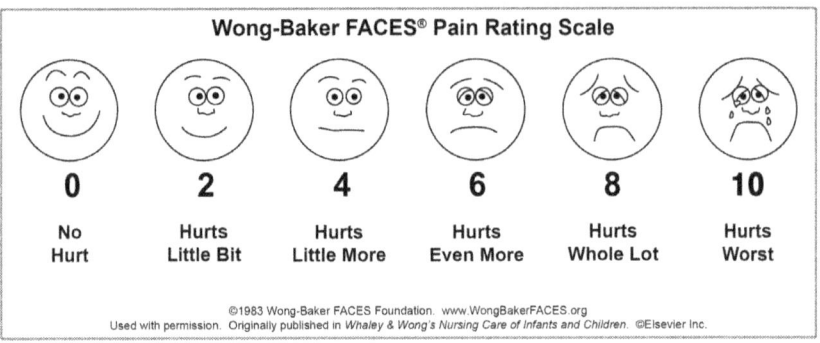

Figure 10. A familiar graphic found in medical offices when asking about level of pain.

Beginning with a negative re-experience ranking 4 or less will allow the mind to reason through the process (as opposed to shutting down and not being able to reach the frontal cortex); in other words, a learning cycle can be completed. So, let's say that one day I walk into an office space that is shared by a number of other colleagues and one particular colleague is putting off negative vibes. I return for several more days and the same vibes are given off. After a week of these experiences, I begin to create a narrative that I'm doing something to cause negative reactions. I make attempts to create an upbeat atmosphere the next week and the vibe doesn't improve. I, intuitively, rank the experience as a level 4 issue; in comparison, my personal logic is this is not a family issue—likely 8 or above rank, this is not an issue with a store cashier—likely a 2 rank. Now what?

On a Problem-Solution T-Map, like seen in figure 11, it's helpful to layout a visual depiction of the problem and recalled solution to maintain focus. The problem experience is "bad vibes at work" and the solution memory is "create positive conclusions."

Problem	Solution
Bad vibes at work	Create Positive Conclusions

Figure 11. Problem-Solution T-Map.

Before getting into more detail, for those interested in technical terms in the mind over matter area, this could be considered a type of Neurolinguistic Programming collapsing technique (visualizing the negative then switching to re-visualizing how a similar problem has been effectively solved in the past).

The following is a simulation of a problem-solution dialogue:

(Facilitator) "Rank 'bad vibes at work' from zero to 10."

(Client) "Four."

(Facilitator) "Okay. Verbalize the problem experience or think about it in your mind. I don't need to hear the explanation of your experience if you prefer not to share."

(Client) Silence and client remembers.

(Facilitator) "Now. Go to the 'create positive conclusions' memory. Elevate this experience; remember where you are, who you are discussing this with, what type of day it is, any other sensations... Remember how you feel when you realize that creating narratives that don't exist are a waste of energy."

(Client) Silence and client remembers.

(Facilitator) "Now. Notice how this feels in the body. Where do you feel the aha, the relief that comes from re-understanding where your energy is best spent?"

(Client) "In my chest, I am breathing easily. In my face, my features are relaxed then I'm smiling. I feel free from taking on the responsibility to elevate others' moods. If others are in a space that is negative then that's where they are. I don't have to take extra steps, feel stressed, or feel like I've done something wrong because someone is in a negative space."

(Facilitator) "Excellent. Go back to the 'bad vibes at work' memory. Stay on that specific example only. Now move quickly and re-experience, in detail, 'create positive conclusions'."

(Client) Silence and client remembers.

(Facilitator) "Go back to the problem. Now experience the solution in great detail."

(Client) Silence and client remembers.

(Facilitator) "Now. Re-experience that specific problem in as much detail as possible. Give me a number on the specific 'bad vibes at work' problem."

(Client pauses, thinks, and responds) "It feels almost silly now that I spent so much time making up stories on what could be wrong and what my role in that was. It's a zero."

For those interested in adding meridian tapping (Emotional Freedom Technique), it's very easy to add tapping while working through the problem-solution format. In my book, *Healing What's Real: Expanding Your Personal Power with Mind Over Matter Techniques*, there is an entire chapter dedicated to Emotional Freedom Technique ("Subconscious Touch Communication—Emotional Freedom Technique"). There are countless free videos on the internet on Emotional Freedom Technique as well (including on my website).

Once getting a hang of the process, it's much easier to transition to higher ranking, negative experiences. When self-facilitating, voice recording the experience may be helpful for those who are more attracted to audio learning, or freewriting for those who are more visual or hands-on. To combine the two, voice dictating can be used with word processing software or an app can be used on cellular phones for no additional cost.

While I've laid out a process, there are times when protocol must be revised. For instance, figure 10 suggests a way to rank emotional duress, the next step would be to collapse the duress with a positive re-association, and re-check the ranking in hopes that it will be lower. However, I have had clients who, instead, identified (or T-Mapped) a problem and a positive re-association, recalled the step-by-step approach to creating positive results, then—like a template—strategized on how those effective steps could be applied to the problem in detail in a session (out loud or silently).

The bigger picture idea is to decrease emotional duress of a recurring theme in addition to becoming resolved on specific experiences during a session. Clients (and now readers) are taught how to use the *Positive Hypnosis* process to empower them to self-collapse specific triggers that show up that aren't addressed in a session (all problems connected to a core issue won't be recalled in a two-hour time-frame).

Returning to the world after a session, recurring events show up and anchors can be recalled quickly to collapse the level of emotional duress in the moment. For instance, if one has the tendency to create narratives that don't exist, this is a daily pattern. Recalling and reusing "create positive conclusions" whenever this pattern emerges collapses the level of the problem. Theoretically, enough work is completed in a controlled environment to decrease negative emotions when real events take place, so blocks aren't holding back positive decision-making that satisfy core needs; re-associations (from the back cortex) pass the amygdala and reasoning can commence in the frontal integrative cortex (a learning cycle can be completed).

Conclusion and Next Steps

What's interesting about thinking, in the purest sense, is not one person thinks exactly alike. All have re-associations that are unique to their personal experiences. So, when someone says, "I know what you're thinking," what is really meant is, "I am attempting to use my past memories (re-associations) to get close enough to your re-associations, so that we can have an approximate meeting of the minds."

The technical learning cycle is a bit more straightforward, however, in the human mind. Scientific research continues to advance on how the brain works, but the idea that re-association is a key to productive re-habiting is a reasonable theory. For professionals who interact with people or those interested in self-facilitation, one, two, or all steps in the *Positive Hypnosis* process may take time to digest and embrace. Make an attempt to become familiar with the protocol outlined, later make adjustments to fit thinking from an individual perspective.

Decide how *Positive Hypnosis* fits by using the templates that apply to each step. Once all materials are sitting on the table, budget 2 to 3, uninterrupted hours, and follow the suggested order. Notice when struggles arise for a particular process, go back to the sections, re-read instructions and simulated examples, revisit steps, and give them another go. While steps may be revised over time, focus must always remain in place—the core need or theme of a session must be consistent. Additional clarity may arise once memories are collected and core need phrasing may be revised, but a clear theme should remain in place to collapse negative patterns (the last step).

When I began putting these puzzle pieces together in graduate school, what became eye-opening to me is that I could apply the learning cycle and re-association concepts to any professional or life scenario. While the process has been shared within the context of Hypnosis, Self-Hypnosis and Neuro-linguistic Programming, knowing how the brain learns and why blocks occur, and that re-association is a key to individual thinking has changed my private practice protocol, the way I teach at the college level, and how I communicate day-to-day.

Armed with more complete understanding, the *woo woo*, perception of being controlled, quack-like-a-duck-on-stage perceptions disappear from one's mind. Re-using memories is a natural process to complete learning cycles and positive habits. *Positive Hypnosis* is simply adding structure around the re-association reality to effectively find solutions. Individual empowerment becomes very clear with this process; people (with healthy human brains) hold the internal key to re-knowing how to achieve their personal well-being. The power lies with effective re-associations.

Sources

Gamboa, Hugo, creator of EEG tracings, Dec. 2005, Creative Commons Attribution-Share Alike 3.0 Accessed 5 September 2017 at Wikimedia Commons.

Wong-Baker FACES Foundation (2017). *Wong-Baker FACES ® Pain Rating Scale,* 2017. Accessed 5 September 2017 with permission from http://www.WongBakerFACES.org.

Zull, James E. *The Art of Changing the Brain: Enriching the Practice of Teaching by Exploring the Biology of Learning.* Sterling, 2002.

Definition of Terms

Anchor: In essence, anchors are perceptions. An anchor is a current belief that is connected to a person, place or thing. A simple example is when a child falls but is not injured; the reaction or anchor re-associates with "I'm hurt" now cry. If a parent kisses the knee to reframe the perception or anchor, the child stops crying once the knee is kissed.

Collapse: Breaking down a habit that no longer serves a positive need.

Core Need: A theme that must play out in a person's life to create fulfillment.

Emotional Freedom Technique (EFT): Releasing negative emotional charges by tapping on specific nerve ending areas on the body to reframe mind/body perceptions.

Feeling Emotions in the Body (also called Acupressure Hypnosis): Noticing how areas of the body react when experiencing specific emotions with the goal of aligning those sensations to create calm and enhance performance. Also see "Hypnosis, Self-Hypnosis, Past Life Regression."

Hypnosis | Self-Hypnosis | Acupressure Hypnosis | Past Life Regression: Finding experiences in connection with the past or present while the mind is in a relaxed state. Collecting information can be accomplished with eyes open or closed.

Mind Over Matter: Recollecting memories to build willpower to overcome problems.

Motor Output: Action taken. The motor movement is a physical decision to either move or not move (even a decision not to move is an action).

Neuro-Linguistic Programming (NLP): A model that connects the relationships between successful patterns of behavior and personal experiences. Connections are made to all levels of communication to enhance recall of personal experiences—verbally (which is less than 10% of what is truly being communicated) and non-verbally (tonality and body language being more than 90% of communication). Also see "Anchor."

Narrative: A story or events spoken, written, or visualized.

Past Lives or Past Life Regression: Incarnations that are re-accessed through visualization. These incarnations are places in history recalled that can be true Past Lives that have been experienced by those visualizing, familial memories that have been buried in the visualizers' DNA (stories told by family, or information patterns are simply buried in DNA), or they are places in history that create vibrant enough narratives to have emotional charges.

Positive Hypnosis: A structure that aids in recalling positive memories (or re-associating) to problem-solve. This revolves around the premise that people (with healthy human brains) hold the internal key to re-knowing how to achieve their personal well-being.

Positive Re-association: Recalling past experiences that contribute to thinking on the bright side of life.

Protocol: The order or process.

Rank / Ranking: A grading system. A hierarchy.

Re-associations: Individual memories.

Reflection (Area): Thoughts stored in the brain.

Re-habit: Re-using memories found in the subconscious that form positive habits.

Satisfaction:: Fulfillment of one's needs or expectations.

Self-facilitate: Performing alone. Self-organizing technical processes.

Simulate: Imitate or produce a performance.

Solution-based: Finding encouraging experiences to create constructive life strategies.

About the Author

Photo by Pat Barcas

Michelle began to better understand the importance of targeting interests and needs of individuals through writing and creative pursuits in corporate America beginning in 1985. Mind, body, soul health became a more pressing need when she decided to strike out on her own in 1996 as a Wholistic Professional and Writer. She was led to Asheville, NC in 2009 where her roots date back to the 1700's. This is where she established a successful wholistic and integrative practice and collaborations that focus on clients, students and communities finding their voices.

In addition, Michelle is a college instructor specializing in English studies and College Transfer Success.

Michelle has an eclectic background with **mind over matter solutions specialties** that include: Doctor of Clinical Hypnosis / Hypnotherapy, Self-Hypnosis, EFT (Emotional Freedom Technique), NLP (Neuro-Linguistic Programming), Acupressure Hypnosis, Past Life Regression, and Writing Coaching. Her **academic work** includes: teaching college English and College Transfer Success, a Master of Arts in English specializing in Rhetoric, Composition and Professional and Technical Writing, a Bachelor of Arts degree in Communication Arts, and various writing projects in academia. Other studies include how personality patterns are influenced by Astrology, Numerology, and Birth Order.

More information on Michelle's background, books, events, community collaborations, teaching, and her private practice can be found at www.MichellePayton.com, www.MichellePaytonWriter.com, www.TheLeftSide.com, or do an internet search on "Michelle Payton." She, her husband and life partner since 1982, and two of three grown children live, work and play in Asheville, North Carolina.

Conscious Living and Self-Help Books by M. A. (Michelle) Payton

As a mind over matter solutions professional and academic, Michelle's work focuses on how to accomplish 21st century, mindful living as a mainstream, as conscious as possible, work-in-progress parent, partner, professional, and individual, and how this has unfolded for her, her clients and throughout history.

About the Author

Adventures of a Mainstream Metaphysical Mom: Choosing Peace of Mind in a World of Diverse Ideas (Book 1)

Mainstream metaphysical parenting, mentoring, and relationships with self and others in the 21st century!

2003 Finalist for Best Biographical/Self-Help Book
—Coalition of Visionary Resources, 2003 Visionary Awards, International New Age Trade Show

192 pp ~ paperback
ISBN 978-0-9719804-0-2
$13.95

"Soul"utions: Achieving Financial, Intellectual, Physical, Social, and Spiritual Balance with Soul

Tips on soul-based living using goal setting principles in all areas of life!

239 pp ~ paperback
ISBN 978-0-9719804-1-9
$14.95

Birth Mix Patterns™: *Astrology, Numerology, and Birth Order, and their Effects on the Past, Present, and Future*

Analyzes hundreds of historical figures, including United States Presidents and First Ladies, artists, authors, civil rights leaders, and more in connection with astrology, numerology, and birth order.

2006 Finalist for Best General Interest/How To Book

—Coalition of Visionary Resources, 2006 Visionary Awards, International New Age Trade Show

160 pp ~ paperback

ISBN: 978-0-9719804-2-6

$12.95

Birth Mix Patterns™: *Astrology, Numerology, and Birth Order, and their Effects on the Families & Other Groups that Matter*

Analyzes the authors of the Declaration of Independence, dark leaders, the US Supreme Court Justices, the Beatles and more in connection with astrology, numerology, and birth order.

133 pp ~ paperback

ISBN 978-0-9719804-3-3

$12.95

Birth Mix Patterns™ and Loving Relationships using Astrology, Numerology, and Birth Order

Analyzes more than two dozen famous couples from Hollywood, to community servers, to same gender partnerships in connection with astrology, numerology, and birth order.

137 pp ~ paperback
ISBN 978-0-9719804-4-0
$12.95

Healing What's Real: Expanding Your Personal Power with Mind Over Matter Techniques

Dr. Payton shares her experiences with Hypnotherapy, Neuro-Linguistic Programming™ (NLP), Emotional Freedom Technique™ (EFT), meditation, and more with dozens of transcribed sessions and interviews combining these techniques.

253 pp ~ paperback
ISBN 978-0-9719804-5-7
$15.95

More Adventures of a Mainstream Metaphysical Mom: Finding Peace While Raising Teens, Building a Community, and Consciously Following-Through (Book 2)
More on mainstream metaphysical parenting, mentoring, and relationships as she and her family age and wade through constant changes and few hard and fast rules.
225 pp ~ paperback
ISBN-13: 978-0-9719804-6-4
$12.95

Writing Sensorably: How Expressive and Natural Voice Advance Recording Thoughts
Those interested in ways to record as much content as possible prior to the polish stage of a final document can begin with the natural speaking voice. Processes shared marry natural expression with practical steps that enhance: self-help processing, scientific observations, creative writing, journaling, descriptive work using multiple senses, and technical or methodical work with an interest in how published papers and research support out-of-the-box processes.
131 pp ~ paperback, ISBN-13: 978-0-9719804-7-1, $13.95
131 pp ~ Kindle Edition (e-book), ISBN-13: 978-09719804-8-8, $6.99

Index

A

ALPHA 16, 17, 28, 34
amygdala 14, 15, 48
Anchor 26, 27, 28, 39, 40, 52, 53

B

BETA 16
block 8, 10, 21
brain 7, 8, 9, 11, 12, 13, 14, 18, 19, 22, 27, 49, 50, 53
brain processing 12
brainwaves 16, 17, 28
brain works 49

C

collapse / collapsing 20, 21, 27, 31, 33, 34, 35, 36, 37, 42, 43, 45, 47, 50
Core Need 22, 24, 26, 27, 38, 43, 52
cortex 9, 10, 12, 14, 15, 18, 19, 20, 21, 44, 48

D

DELTA 17

E

EFT / Emotional Freedom Technique 46, 52
emotions 14, 24, 27, 37, 47, 52

F

fight-flight-freeze 9, 12
frontal integrative cortex 10, 14, 15, 19, 48

H

habit 7, 8, 15, 18, 20, 21, 22, 23, 27, 31, 42, 52, 53
hypnosis 1, 3, 7, 8, 12, 16, 20, 21, 22, 30, 31, 47, 49, 50, 52, 53

I

intuition / intuitive 43, 44

L

learning cycle 7, 9, 10, 11, 12, 13, 14, 15, 18, 19, 21, 34, 44, 48, 49, 50
level of pain 44

M

mind over matter 2, 46, 52
motor output 53

N

narrative 26, 39, 53
NLP / Neuro-linguistic Programming 7, 8, 12, 20, 22, 33, 45, 50

P

Past Lives / Past Life Regression 30, 31, 32, 52, 53
Positive Hypnosis 7, 12, 16, 21, 30, 31, 47, 49, 50, 53
Positive Re-association 53
problem-solving 30
protocol 7, 20, 30, 47, 49, 50, 53

R

rank / ranking 34, 44, 47
Re-association 9, 14, 18, 53
reflection 9, 14, 15, 18, 20
re-habit 18, 45

Index

S

satisfaction 22, 23, 33, 38, 42

self-facilitate / self-facilitation 22, 27, 28, 34, 36, 46, 48, 54

Self-Hypnosis 7, 8, 16, 20, 22, 50, 52, 56

simulate 24, 35, 43, 49

solution-based 7, 21, 38

T

temporal integrative cortex 9, 10, 14

THETA 17

T-Map 33, 35, 44, 45, 47

trance 16, 17

W

Weiss, Brian 30

Z

Zull, James 12

www.ingramcontent.com/pod-product-compliance
Lightning Source LLC
Chambersburg PA
CBHW051716040426
42446CB00008B/919